life.
GAME ON!

a competitor's guide

DANI GOLDEN

Crystal Pointe Media, Inc.
San Diego, CA

LIFE.GAME ON!
A Competitor's Guide
By Dani Golden

Copyright © 2015 Dani Golden

Published by Crystal Pointe Media, Inc.
San Diego, California

ISBN: 978-0-692-53063-4

Cover Design by Chris Lugo
Interior Layout by Nick Zelinger

First Edition

Printed in the United States of America

To anyone who has ever struggled with competition.
This one's for you!

Acknowledgements

Competition is something I have battled with my entire life. Naturally a more sensitive person, I felt everything. I needed to learn how to better navigate my emotions and manage them. If I could learn to do that, I could master my world and excel at anything I put my mind and heart to.

Of course, my journey would not have been complete without the loving support of my mother and father. Not only did they love me unconditionally but wanted what was best for me. Fun, laughter, and happiness were and still are the most important goals I should aspire to. After all, a gold medal can only do so much. After the crowd's cheers and the time in the spotlight has faded, it's the moments by yourself, the ones no one else sees but your close friends and family members, that offer the most glory. These are the moments I have learned to cherish and hold dearly.

When it comes to finding ourselves, growing and learning how best to navigate life and its obstacles, it is imperative that you surround yourselves with your biggest cheerleaders.

The people who truly want to see you grow and shine. The people who will never ask you to dim your light. No, the special people who are responsible for where I am today, were and are essential on my journey. My gratitude is immense and my appreciation overwhelming. Thank you. I dedicate this book to you and all my gracious readers who like me, just want to find a way to engage in competition in a healthy way. To your silent wins. May they make the loudest impact in your lives and help inspire you to keep fighting for you.

In a world that never sleeps
Competition will find you and your ambitions
Fears will sink in and negative emotions will creep
The challenge is to shine and be the best you
Be the person you've dreamed about becoming,
Grow and Bloom
Should people come into your sphere and surround
you with doubt and toxic glue
Remember to keep moving as nothing can hold you
back
Dream, hold on to your ambitions, work hard and
stay true
In the end the Game of Life is your journey
Isn't it time to be the best YOU!

Contents

Introduction 1

Defining Competition 7

What Is Competition? 13

Two Types of Competition 19

Healthy Competition vs.
    Unhealthy Competition 21

Competition in Sports 33

Competition in Business 39

Competition Among Friends 53

Suppressing Your Competitive Spirit. 59

Competition and Doubt 67

Competition and Fear 75

Competition and Anger 79

Competition and Social Media. 85

Competition and Motivation 93

Gaining a Competitive Advantage. 99

Conclusion 119

Introduction

My name is Dani Golden. I am a champion Olympic swimmer. I went to my first Olympics in 1992 when I was only 13 years old and I was the youngest person ever to qualify. I won a gold medal in every individual event I swam and all my times shattered world records. Every relay team I was on came in first place. I was the first swimmer to bring home more gold medals than Mark Spitz. You are probably thinking that's amazing and are wondering why you don't recognize my name. The reason you don't know me and haven't heard about any of my triumphs is because none of this ever really happened. The only place these events actually occurred was in my very active imagination.

The truth is, I did grow up swimming competitively, and my dream was to be an Olympic swimmer. My family didn't have a pool so I used to put on my swimsuit, cap and goggles, and pretend I was swimming in our living room. I would imagine the excitement in the voices of the announcers as they described my race. They would talk about how great my stroke looked or how talented I was, especially when it came to competing. This was one of the ways I embraced competition.

Competition has been an on-going theme in my life. I've even had someone jokingly refer to me as Seabiscuit. I used to argue with her and say, "No, I'm not Seabiscuit. I'm Secretariat." She would then go on and provide me with examples as to why my competitive style was more like Seabiscuit than Secretariat. She was right. I was the underdog.

We are all competitive creatures. We have goals and dreams that we wish to fulfill, but sometimes our way of dealing with competition can get in the way. Because competition is constantly playing peek-a-boo in our lives, we find ourselves having to manage our emotions and our actions as they relate to our competitive nature. Competition in its various forms has definitely thrown me off my game several times throughout my life. That is why I want to discuss how we can promote a healthier competitive atmosphere in all phases of our lives.

Healthy competition is my imagining fulfilling my Olympic dreams. Harmless visualization tactics like these help us to continue to strive for greatness. Competition allows us to define what we want.

It provides us with the opportunity to be passionate and have fun. A healthy competitor does not lose focus when faced with unavoidable distractions or challenging setbacks.

Why is understanding competition important? The world is competitive, and so are we are. Competition is not just something that we do in sports. It permeates our lives. It's there when we wake up in the morning and get dressed. We select our clothes based on our mood and how we want to present ourselves to the world that day. We distinctly brand ourselves and we do this because we want to be seen as unique individuals. Competition is also present in your interactions with friends. You may not realize it, but when you get together with friends you quickly do a once-over and size them up. Don't lie. That's competing. Comparing is competing.

Social media is also a mecca for comparison and competition. How many friends, likes, posts, and followers do you have? Where did you travel lately? Look at my Instagram. Look at how happy I am at this concert. I'm having the time of my life. Where are you? Logging on is like opting into a competition you did not sign up for, yet you feel as though you have to play. Why? What's the point? It's not like you actually win anything. In fact, you may be losing. By focusing on our online presence, we can easily forget to enjoy our offline moments. We compete with one another for so many things without realizing it, and then we wonder why certain activities, which hardly take any effort, end up making us feel so exhausted. We're exhausted because while we've been engaging in these activities, we've been silently competing.

The other day I was competing with the clock. It's silly, I know! I was getting anxious about having my book ready, and I wanted everything done yesterday. Well, that wasn't possible. Yet I was driving myself crazy competing with an inanimate object that doesn't know I exist and doesn't care. The clock is still going to move forward whether I like it or not. This is a form of unhealthy competition, when we try to control things that are completely out of our control. Do you realize how exhausting engaging in this type of behavior can be? Gossiping and bullying are also forms of unhealthy competition. They suck the life out of us. It's not just emotionally draining but time consuming. Putting others down to feel better about yourself is not a productive way to spend your time. Negative behavior brought on by unsettling emotions makes us feel like we're spinning our wheels sprinting for the end zone. Caught out of breath, we've forgotten our purpose.

Competition is a crazy maze, and sometimes trying to navigate it can be tricky. That is why I'd like you to think about the following question. If there is such a thing as healthy competition, what are its characteristics and how do we define it?

Defining Competition

L et me start by saying that I am not a psychologist. I am just an individual who has grown up in today's society, who was exposed to competition at an early age. I took my first steps in a baby pool, and that's all it took for me to know that I loved the water and I loved swimming. My parents supported my passion. Never focused on winning or losing, they only cared about whether I was having fun. I, on the other hand, was born competitive. I've tried denying it, but I have learned that gets me nowhere.

Merriam-Webster's Dictionary defines *competition* as "the act or process of trying to get or win something (such as a prize or a higher level of success) that someone else is also trying to get or win." Now, let's think about that for a second. Does there need to be someone else who is also trying to get or win something for competition to exist? It seems to me that there are two schools of thought. The primitive school of thought believes that resources are limited to a chosen few. These people secretly wish for others to fail just so that they can succeed. Because they ascribe to this scarcity of resources theory, they find themselves being competitive with everyone, even if it makes no sense. For example, they might work a nine-to-five job that they kind of like, and they have a friend who's ambitious and passionate about being a comedian. Rather than encouraging their friend and building them up, they live in the land of practicality on the verge of negativity. They assume their friend won't be successful because why should they? Only a few people make it big as comedians. How can their friend actually think that it's going to be them?

The second school of thought is more New Age. It's the type of thinking based on the concept that there is more than enough to go around. This is called the law of attraction—that thinking positively will bring positive results. There is no scarcity of resources. People who embrace this philosophy believe that other people's achievements do not diminish their own ability to shine. They are happy when they see their friends dreaming and acting on their dreams.

The word *competition* comes from the Latin *competitio*, which means "rivalry." The English word evolved from the word *compete*. *Merriam-Webster's Dictionary* defines the word *compete* as "to try to get or win something (such as a prize or reward) that someone else is also trying to win: to try to be better or more successful than someone or something else: to try to be noticed, accepted, or chosen over something else." As you can see, the definitions for *competition* and *compete* are almost identical, except *competition* doesn't include the desire to be noticed, accepted or chosen over something else. What's even more interesting is that the word *compete* comes from the Latin verb *competere*, which means "to seek together, to come together, agree, be suitable." So how did coming together, agreeing and being suitable evolve into what we know today as competition; the kind of competition that distances people from one another as opposed to the kind that creates camaraderie?

In both biology and sociology, competition is a contest between organisms, animals, individuals, or groups, for a variety of things. These could include territory, a niche, resources, goods, mates, prestige, recognition, awards, group or social status. So, scientifically speaking, it would seem that we're programmed to be competitive, and that the evolution of competition we see today is no different than that demonstrated in the past. It's just the semantics that got twisted.

Why is any of this important? Competition is everywhere and it affects us all. As I mentioned earlier, I was born competitive. I have an older brother. When we were kids, I used to chase him around and try to insert myself in every activity he engaged in with his friends. I always wanted to be included, and when I was, I never wanted to be the one with the least amount of talent or skills. When we used to play hide and seek, I would get so nervous about being found that I would pee a little. My adrenaline would be pumping and all I knew was that I had to get past my competitor without getting tagged and make it to the safe zone.

Competition can bring out the best and the worst in us. People often say that if you really want to get to know someone, play golf with them. Having never played golf, I can't verify that statement. I can, however, acknowledge that someone's character can be gauged as a result of their behavior based on their performance. As a child, I would throw temper tantrums when I would lose. My mother hated it, of course. She didn't understand where it came from and wished her beautiful daughter wouldn't react in such an ugly way. My reaction came from within. While I don't want to lump myself into the bad sportsmanship category, my behavior controlled me. Too young to make sense of my competitive emotions, I did not understand the powerful feelings

I would have when I wasn't proud of my performances. These feelings were the result of my competitive nature. I wanted to do my best and was frustrated that I couldn't control the situation, ignore my negative thoughts and block out all external distractions.

What Is Competition?

W e've already defined the word competition, but what is competition as it relates to us? When I was 10, my family moved from New Jersey to San Diego. I distinctly recall the details because it was the middle of fifth grade. The first day I attended my new school, I wore a jean outfit with penny loafers. I remember walking to class and feeling embarrassed because I realized how different I looked. No one else was wearing jeans. The other girls had on bright, neon colored shorts with t-shirts or tank tops and tennis shoes or sandals. Clearly, I stood out. I was ostracized and teased because I didn't dress like they did, and to top it off, I had a New Jersey accent. I was different, and being different can create a competitive environment. Anxious to place me in some stereo-typical box, the other students wanted to know where I was from, if I was athletic or smart, and if the boys would think that I was pretty.

The one place I knew I wouldn't have a problem fitting in, was the pool. I joined my first club swim team, and quickly realized how much more competitive swimming was in California. That summer I remember getting in trouble for participating in Junior Lifeguards before I came to afternoon swim practice. My coach was mad at me because she thought that I was wasting my time and my talent doing something other than swimming. Rather than talking to me about it, she tasked me with more dry land exercises than my peers, placed me in my own lane and gave me a more difficult workout. She was punishing me for having other interests and I was only 11 years old! Now this was southern California competitive swimming.

Competition doesn't just exist in sports—it exists everywhere. Women compete with other women to be smarter and more attractive, and men do the same. We spend endless amounts of time and energy competing with our peers without them even knowing. We compare ourselves to our friends and family, and we even compete with strangers. Whether conscious or subconscious, we have a constant need to know where we stand in relation to others. When did we stop focusing on ourselves? It would be one thing if we found inspiration in playing this comparison game, but we don't. Instead we pick ourselves apart, over analyze our actions and create self-inflicted wounds, steering us away from our goals and weakening our sense of self.

When I graduated from high school, I had absolutely
no idea where I wanted to go to college. I was scared,
and I felt lost. Looking around at my peers, it seemed
as if everyone else knew exactly what they wanted to
do and where they wanted to go. They had direction.
I, on the other hand, had absolutely none. I remember
wondering what was wrong with me. Where was my
direction, my path? I spent an exorbitant amount of
time comparing myself to my friends and my peers,
and in doing so I kept feeling worse about myself.
Being the odd man out was lonely. My mom tried
to convince me that I wasn't alone. She told me my
friends probably felt the same way, but just weren't
being as open as I was in talking about it. I didn't
believe her. They all seemed so sure.

I wasn't just competing with my friends academically;
I spent much of my adolescent years competing with
my friends for my own individual style. There's a
reason fashion is a billion dollar industry; what we
wear and how we decide to dress is our way of
presenting ourselves to the world. Our clothes are an
extension of our personality. It's our way of standing
out and differentiating ourselves. When I was a kid,
I remember getting upset when my girlfriends would
buy the exact same outfit as I did. I know that they
say imitation is the sincerest form of flattery, but I just

found it annoying. In my opinion, copying someone else's style is something that a person does when they can't think for themselves. Why does it bother me so much? People want to be unique, and I am no different. Our attire affords us the ability to creatively express ourselves. If everyone looks the same, it defeats the purpose. By stealing the "look" I had put together, my friends were saying there was nothing special about me; they could recreate what I had done.

Dressing to be different and wanting to establish our own identity is not necessarily unhealthy competitive behavior. It doesn't mean we're being malicious or undermining others. It's simply one way of expressing ourselves. Sometimes this competitive spirit gets inspired from within, like when we wear our "go to outfit" that boosts our confidence every time we put it on. Other times it occurs when others inspire and challenge us. For example, we see a cute dress or blazer in a magazine, and buy something similar to accent our wardrobe and make us feel refreshed and refined from the moment we purchase it. Whether inspired by others or from within, our behavior reflects how we're programmed and how we react to certain circumstances.

While competition impacts much of the world we live in, it's also proven to be a popular theme for escape. Look at TV shows like *The Bachelor, Survivor, The Amazing Race, American Idol* and *American Ninja Warrior.* All of these shows are based on competition, and we enjoy watching them. We love watching people shine, but we also find ourselves getting sucked into the drama as we watch contestants interact with one another. We find their competitive nature—the drama of competition—fascinating. In a way, we're all anthropologists—people watchers amused and intrigued by the behavior of others. I most certainly am. While I'm more of a fan of competition shows on the Food Network like *Chopped*, we all have our guilty pleasures.

There's nothing wrong with being entertained by competition. We enjoy cheering on the underdogs or the nice guys and seeing the bad guys take a beating. It feels good to see justice delivered. At least, that's how I see it. What you will notice when you watch these types of shows, however, is that the nice guy doesn't always finish first. I'll be watching *Chopped* and there will be some egocentric, narcissistic chef bad-mouthing his competitors. I'll be rooting for him to be chopped, and unfortunately, he will win. That's the interesting thing about competition; it's often unpredictable, and can be less subjective than you would like to think. While there are definitely sports and art forms that lend themselves to public opinion, as opposed to finite performance times, there is an evident skill and grace presented by certain contestants that is visible and unquestionable. The best performer will be the better competitor, sometimes despite their personality. That's how competition works. Unless we're talking about a popularity contest, it doesn't matter who's the most liked. What matters is which competitor is able to outshine the others and excel at their craft in a way that their competitors cannot.

So if we revisit *Merriam-Webster Dictionary's* definition of *competition*, it would seem that competition clearly includes being better than someone else. The next questions that concern us then are: how do we manage our competitive nature and what is healthy competition?

Two Types of Competition

In biology, there are two main types of competition, *interspecific* and *intraspecific*. They exist in every competitive situation. Sometimes they coexist, and other times one is more dominant than the other.

Interspecific competition occurs when two or more people compete for the same thing. There's a game we used to play in Junior Lifeguards called "Beach Flags." It was one of my favorites. Multiple competitors line up in a row with their stomachs on the sand and their arms folded so that their chin is resting on their hands. The flags are placed about twenty-five yards behind the competitors'. There are fewer flags than there are competitors. As soon as you hear, "ready, set, go," you quickly push yourself to your feet, turn around and sprint to try to capture one of the beach flags. Since there are fewer flags than there are competitors, the people who do not capture a flag are eliminated. This process continues until there is one man left standing. Beach Flags is an example of interspecific competition. Much like musical chairs, interspecific competition relies on other people in order for competition to exist.

Now that we've talked about interspecific competition, let's discuss intraspecific competition. When you compete with yourself, you are engaging in intraspecific competition. While there have been times in my childhood when I competed more with others than with myself, as I grew older I realized that I performed much better when I was competing with myself. This did not mean that I wasn't aware of my opponents or did not acknowledge them. It just meant that my biggest motivator was my own competitive spirit, and my desire to continually improve in an area, whether it was in academics or in sports. Some people are good at pushing themselves and setting goals. They're inspired by their competitors and perform well when they race against them, but their primary engine is their inner motivation. Many runners and swimmers talk about PR in a race, or a personal record. Their whole objective is to beat their own time. Rather than focusing on how they finish in relation to others, they focus on themselves. For them it's not about winning or losing but about achieving a personal best time.

Regardless of whether you're an interspecific or intraspecific competitor or both, what matters is that you find a way to engage in healthy competition. What is healthy competition? I had that exact same question.

Healthy Competition vs. Unhealthy Competition

Growing up, I always considered myself to be a tomboy, extremely athletic and boisterous. My dad used to call me "Buster," as in, the number-one ball buster. One night when I was about four years old, he brought home a yellow t-shirt with ironed-on letters. It had my name, *Dani*, and right below that, #1 *Buster*. My dad begged me to put on the shirt, but I refused. It wasn't until he stopped asking and had forgotten about it that I appeared in the living room doorway, dancing while wearing the yellow t-shirt. This was my competitive spirit in action. I was adamant about having the upper hand. I still have that same stubborn attitude today, and I love that part of me. While my competitive nature has made some things more difficult for me, I'd say that overall, it has served me well.

Being competitive, however, can have an ugly connotation in our society. It has become in some ways synonymous with greed, envy, and narcissism, which is one of the reasons I found myself trying to deny my competitive nature. My competitiveness made me feel uncomfortable. Sometimes I would have these negative and mean thoughts. I didn't like them. I struggled with wanting to play nice with others but also wanting to stand out. The competitor inside me didn't want to be like everyone else. Then again, who does? We all want to be individuals with unique characteristics and talents that help formulate our sense of self, who we are and how we are perceived.

When competition is unhealthy, competitive thoughts tend to be exaggerated, unsettling thoughts. Sometimes I would voice these thoughts only to my mom and my therapist. One day, my mom threw me off by asking an interesting question. She asked me why others had to fail for me to succeed. That question made my stomach churn. I stood there in silence, contemplating what she had just said. She was right. Why did others have to perform worse than I did for me to feel special? It wasn't that I was getting off on other people's misery, but I did feel the need to be better than others. I voiced this epiphany to my therapist who then asked me another interesting question, what is healthy competition?

While most people might not want to consider themselves "competitive," being competitive is actually healthy. Being competitive allows us to connect with our wants, needs and desires. It allows us to dream big and break glass ceilings. The problem happens when people are uncomfortable with their competitive thoughts and deem them unacceptable. They suppress these emotions and feelings, which in turn can end up being emotionally harmful to themselves and others. This is why it is important that we learn to own our emotions. Rather than running from them, we should accept them and know that having competitive thoughts or feelings is completely natural. It's how we're programmed. Healthy competition allows us to achieve great things. It enables us to challenge ourselves and push our limits. Whether you're competing with yourself or others, competition needs to exist as it motivates you to be better, do better.

One day I was sitting in my therapist's office talking about competition when she asked me if I'd still be motivated if competition didn't exist. She asked, "If you were an athlete training by yourself, with no game day, no coach, no competitors, no one to see your successes or failures, would you still be motivated?" Initially I said yes. Then I started to think more about her question. I asked myself what motivated me and if an element of that motivation came from comparing myself to others. It did. If you were asked that very same question, what would your answer be? If you were being honest with yourself and accepting of your competitive nature, you too might find yourself responding to that question the same way that I did. Maybe not. I would argue, however, that if you never had anyone to compete or compare yourself to, you might not stay motivated for long. Whether we're competing with others directly or indirectly, there comes a point in time where we seek a frame of reference, an observational way to measure our own abilities and achievements.

When managed in a healthy manner, competition can be invigorating. I mean, why would we even set goals if we weren't motivated to achieve them? Wouldn't staying the same—not moving forward and making progress—take away some of the joy of life? Part of feeling alive, whether an athlete or not, is creating a goal and accomplishing it.

When I first moved to San Diego and joined a club swim team, I was introduced to a variety of new experiences. One of those was the Junior Olympics, which we called J.O.'s. Junior Olympics consists of a competition for swimmers from the age of 10 to the age of 18. The meet lasts three days and consists of prelims and finals. There's even a break between prelims and finals. For a girl from New Jersey, that's a big deal, as it makes the event very special. The Olympics has prelims and finals, and Junior Olympics was the first meet I had gone to that had the same set-up. My goal from the first time I was exposed to Junior Olympics was to win a gold medal. I dreamed of sitting in lane 4 and having my name, Dani Golden, erupt from the loud speaker. "Coming in first and swimming in lane 4 with a time of—MY BEST TIME EVER—is Dani Golden." I would then get out of the pool and accept my gold medal.

For three years and one month, I trained my tail off. I forgot about the announcer and the gold medal and focused on my workouts. I focused on myself. That's healthy competition. There were times, however, when my focus wasn't so great, and I was distracted by fellow teammates. Teammates would be on my feet in workouts and draft off me but never pass me. Teammates would cheat and pretend they were done with a set, even though we both knew that I had lapped them several times. That always irritated me. There was even a teammate of mine whose mom would stand behind my lane and time me. That drove me nuts. Looking back, I suppose I wasn't as mentally tough as I wanted to be. Had I been tougher, her presence would have meant nothing.

As my training continued, there were definitely ups and downs. The biggest challenge for me was not to psyche myself out. I didn't do this in my workouts, but was a master at it when it came to swim meets. Had I known then what I know now, I wouldn't have had that problem. Such is life. Looking back, I am able to see how part of my downs were the result of my engaging in unhealthy competition.

Unhealthy competition makes people do things that they would not admit to a friend or even to themselves. It makes people cut corners and cheat. It uses other people, not as a form of motivation, but as a means to an end. Unhealthy competition is the kind of competition that some of us think of when we deny our competitiveness. It creates such a cringe-worthy feeling that there is no way we would ever want to be associated with it. It's just not us. We're not conniving and mean. We have morals and ethics. We don't believe in using others as stepping stones. We don't take credit for other people's ideas or think of stealing them. We prefer to do things the right way, which is why we do not consider ourselves to be competitive.

Well, news-flash, we're still competitive. We're just not the nasty kind of competitive we loathe. We're engaging in healthy competitive behavior, whereas the people who make our bellies tighten up and surround us with a cloud of negativity, are practicing unhealthy competitive behavior.

What's the difference? Well, one makes us feel good while the other makes us feel icky and just not right. Have you ever done anything to deliberately sabotage someone else? Maybe you let your attractive friend do something stupid so that you'd get the girl or get the guy to ask for your number instead. That's unhealthy competition. It doesn't mean you're a bad person, but it is something that you can control. The reason you don't feel good when you engage in unhealthy competition, is because it's not embracing competition's true spirit. Healthy competition breeds positivity, not negativity. It brings out the best in us. It creates a natural high.

Competition is something that people do to achieve their dreams and conquer their goals. It's the U.S Women's National Soccer Team talking about how fun it is to tear it up together on the soccer field. For such talented women, practice doesn't mean pain-free workouts, but it does mean pushing each other every single day. It also provides these female athletes with a strong connection, a bond, as they help one another through their daily struggles. There's a sense of camaraderie. A study found that social bonding releases more endorphins, and as a result, the athletes who trained together were able to withstand twice as much pain as those who worked out alone. Another study discovered that females who trained with others worked much harder and longer than those who worked out by themselves. Now, that is competition, healthy competition.

I did not experience healthy competition until I was 13 years old. The stars aligned and training became more fun than it had ever been. It's a difficult feeling to describe, but all I can say is that I was no longer in my own way.

I recently recorded a swim meet on TV and saw an interview with Natalie Coughlin. She had just won the 100 meter freestyle. After her swim she was asked what she enjoyed more, competition or practice. She replied, "Practice." She then went on to make a valid point by saying how she couldn't do what she was doing, which was being a competitive swimmer at the top level, had she not loved what she did. Practice took place most days, while competing was a small percentage of her time, so of course she had to love training. In that same vein but on a completely different level, I was approaching swimming in a way that I hadn't done before. I was embracing my training, feeling my own strength, owning my workouts and most importantly, I was only competing with myself. That summer I won the gold medal at Junior Olympics in the 200 meter breaststroke. The irony is that after I won, my mom asked me if it felt as good as I thought it would. I nonchalantly replied, "Not really." It wasn't that it didn't feel good. The race was exhilarating, but it all happened so fast. I had chased this goal for so long and now it was over. So like any other athlete, I cherished it for the time it lasted, but came to practice that following Monday having to start from scratch.

You see, for me, the best part of winning wasn't the medal. It was the race, the journey, being in the zone without even knowing it and "coming to" after that moment had passed. When you're in the zone, you are so involved in what you're doing that your reflexes take over and your actions become automatic. Your mind and body are communicating without your having to deliver the message. That is exactly how I felt. I was whole; I was one. My actions were the sum of all of my parts. With each glide, I was completely involved in what I was doing. My energy was flowing smoothly. There were no thoughts in my mind. I was 100% focused. I was relaxed, energized and every stroke felt comfortable. It felt perfect without me even having to think about it. Looking back, I would almost go so far as to call it a state of euphoria. It was that magical. It was so magical that while I was experiencing being in the zone, I had zero knowledge of it, because I was that in tune.

It's funny. The experience of winning the Junior Olympics teaches me more now than it did then. In 20/20 hindsight, I am able to reflect and realize that the best competitive moments for me were the ones when I was competing with myself, visualizing my races and not paying attention to my competition. Even during that gold medal race, I could hear screams as I made my final turn, warning me that my competition was creeping up fast. All I can remember, however, was how focused and driven I was. I heard the warning, and I took notice. Out of the corner of my right eye, I could see my competition two lanes over catching up to me. Rather than focus on my competitor, I made a mental note and continued my race. That moment taught me the power of using my competitive energy wisely. Had I focused on my competitor, as I had done in the past, all my energy would have been directed toward her, not me. I would have gotten out of sync, my strokes would have been less effective, and my hands would have slipped through the water. This time I was determined not to feel like that. I maintained my focus. This time I used my healthy competitive spirit and focused my energy on me. Don't get me wrong, I still had it in me to win and beat my competition, but my competitive nature looked at that race as an opportunity to achieve a goal. My sole focus wasn't to outperform my competition, but to outperform myself.

In many ways, competition makes us more complex. It helps us grow. As long as competition continues to challenge us and make us strive to be better, it can be joyful. It can stimulate us and keep us motivated. Once competition causes us to focus more on our opponents than on ourselves, we have lost our competitive edge. The enjoyment is gone, and our motivation has changed its course. Rather than trying to enhance our own ability, perfect our swing, our stroke, or our shot, our goal has morphed into one that solely aims to beat the competition.

There were many races in which I placed much higher than those who were more talented or faster because they had a bad race. Did that make me feel special? Not at all. Winning for me was not when I beat my competitors. Winning for me was when I did my best time. It was even sweeter if I was able to touch out a few of my competitors while I was doing it. What was ideal was when my competitors swam their best, and I beat them while I too was swimming my best. That was the ultimate. The point is, healthy competition, just like its origin *compete* and its Latin origin which mentions coming together, brings people together to do their best. While there may be a winner and a loser, the real satisfaction comes from knowing that all competitors performed at their optimal level.

Competition in Sports

The mental aspect of sports should not be under-rated. You know the saying, sports are 90% mental and 10% athletic ability—well I believe it. If what we think affects how we feel, which in turn dictates our actions, how can sports not be 90% mental? This is why developing mental toughness and resilience is something professional athletes have to practice.

Earlier I mentioned how when I swam I used to get in my own way. What I didn't tell you was how emotionally exhausting that was for me. I used to spend hours at swim meets listening to my Walkman (I know I'm dating myself), trying to pump myself up and mentally prepare for my races. I was a really good workout swimmer. My coach even told my mom that if all of his swimmers trained as hard as I did, they'd be Olympians. I cherished that compliment as it validated my hard work. Despite my work ethic during practices, I was an inconsistent competitor. Not including my phenomenal performance at one particular Junior Olympics, I had always been in the top group but never first, second or even third. There was even a period of time when I thought I had the fourth place curse.

Swim meets were not my forte, which was a hard pill to swallow considering I wanted to be an Olympic swimmer. While I set short-term and long-term goals for myself, like winning Junior Olympics, I knew I had to work on my mental state when it came to competition. Athletes need to learn not to psyche themselves out. When someone is too stuck in their own head, the negative thinking and doubt can spiral until they are out of control. I should have spent more time developing a healthy competitive mind that was focused and determined, a mind that wouldn't have listened to all my doubts and succumbed to my fear of failure. I should have harnessed my competitive energy and practiced being competitive with myself, not my competition.

When it comes to competition, there's another saying that illustrates how powerful the mind can be; if you can see it, believe it. My father once told me that winners knew that they were going to win prior to competing. This made a lot of sense to me. My mom would always tell me she could tell how my race was going to be, just by looking at my demeanor on the starting block. Crazy, isn't it? To think that we consciously or subconsciously can seal our own fate even before the competition begins.

Perhaps our fate is influenced by how and why we choose to compete. The term *autotelic* is derived from two Greek words: *auto*, meaning self, and *telos*, meaning goal. The term refers to a self-contained activity where there are no expectations, no ulterior motives. It occurs when someone is doing something simply because they enjoy it, not because they think they're going to get some reward out of it. The activity itself is the reward. Most goals we create are not 100% autotelic. I loved swimming, but I also wanted to be an Olympic swimmer. When something is 100% autotelic, however, it creates a whole different type of experience.

When I was swimming my best, I was thriving in my workouts. I loved training. It did not feel like a chore, and I did not flinch when the coach gave us our main set. I was in the moment. I remember one Saturday morning practice when I was swimming long course, and the sun was beating on my back and the air smelled like summer. I was swimming a freestyle set, just gliding through the water, and watching my reflection on the bottom of the pool. It felt like heaven. The autotelic experience lifts our consciousness to a whole different level. Irritation becomes engagement, doubt dissipates and there is enjoyment in every moment. These are the moments that give athletes a competitive edge. They feel as though they are in control and everything is going to work out. They are 100% focused, invigorated, and alive.

Harnessing the ability to "be in the zone" is a job in and of itself. I am told that it is possible, but that it takes time and practice. One must be willing to venture outside their comfort zone, and not be afraid to challenge old patterns of behavior. Rather than having our energy divided among conflicting thoughts, we need to be able to focus. The optimal experience requires a very active role of the self. For example, when I was swimming my 200 meter breaststroke, I was aware of my stroke and how smooth my movements felt. I was not thinking about whether or not my timing was off or if I should readjust my kick. I was conscious of my actions without judging or analyzing them. I wasn't focusing on my competitors, but only on myself. I did not have the time or the energy for any of the little things that could have affected my performance prior to go time.

Providing athletes with the tools to train their minds to be impenetrable and immune to fellow competitor's attempts at psyching them out, is a necessity. If athletes can learn to control their thoughts and be mindful and aware of them, they can use this technique to their competitive advantage. Just as the physical aspect of sports requires natural talent that is enhanced by practice; the mental aspect of sports must be viewed the same way. Having seen a psychologist for my own personal growth, one of the biggest lessons I've learned is how my thoughts affect my mood and how my mood can dictate my actions. This can be problematic if my mood is negative and I don't acknowledge that I need to make an attitude adjustment. By training my mind and learning to control my thoughts, I can significantly enhance my performance and increase my personal growth.

Competition in Business

We live in a capitalist society. The fundamental nature of business in the United States is predicated on competition. This is nothing new. The question is, how does competition in its various forms affect employees in business? There's a growing trend for companies to go out of their way to support their employees. A great example of this would be Google. In addition to a great benefits package, they provide gourmet food, allow employees to bring pets to work, and offer other perks like access to new technology, a gym, and rides to work. Obviously, someone at Google realized that if they wanted to be successful and attract top talent, they needed to spoil their employees. Why would pandering to your employees matter? It's quite simple really; the happier the employee, the higher the productivity. Think about it for a second. Just like anything in life, a person performs better when they're motivated. The question then remains, how can I motivate my employees? This is not a simple answer as people are motivated by different things. Some people are motivated by money, others by success; some just want to learn, while others want to feel as though they are a part of something bigger. We're all different, so it makes perfect sense that there's no one size fits all when it comes to motivation. Connecting with your employees and anticipating their wants and needs can help CEOs, business owners and key decision-makers motivate their employees so that they can create a rich environment that breeds productivity and innovation.

Healthy competition in business challenges employees to be more innovative. It provides companies and employees with the opportunity to differentiate themselves from their competitors. Healthy competition recognizes that developing ideas, such as providing great customer service, can attract more customers and increase a company's bottom line.

I worked at Nordstrom while in college and briefly after I graduated. There I was able to see firsthand how much of an impact exceptional customer service—a concept that seems so simple and so obvious—could make. I adopted Nordstrom's customer service policy and made it a part of my work ethic, my attitude, my approach and utilized it throughout my professional career. When I worked in Advertising and was presenting proposals to clients, I was thorough. I made sure I had an answer for any question my client could possibly ask. If I did not have the answer, I would tell them that I would do the research and then get back to them in a timely manner. I worked on instilling more efficient workflow policies both internally and with vendors. Looking back, I believe that by incorporating great customer service into my work ethic, I helped separate myself from my competitors and my colleagues. While being spoken of positively was not a goal of mine, being valued was. It was extremely important to me to be on top of my game, proactive and responsible. Had I been more focused on my colleagues as opposed to my work, I would not have been able to perform at the level that I challenged myself to achieve. I set an extremely high bar for myself. I did not have the time nor the mental energy to focus on my competitors. In my mind, I wasn't even competing. I was getting paid to learn. This clearly gave me a competitive edge because it kept me motivated. While the other people were competing for commission, I was working hard, establishing relationships, exceeding expectations and reaping the rewards. As long as I was learning, I was happy. It was only when my supervisors would task me with unnecessary busy work that my motivation would subside. While I always held the attitude that nothing was beneath me and had no problem getting my hands dirty, I unfortunately knew when work was given to me just because, not out of necessity.

Want to demotivate employees? Burying employees with unnecessary busy work while micro managing them in the process, is one surefire way to lose your employees' dedication and commitment. While I'm not saying that bosses and their team need to be friends and sing "Kumbaya," there is a respectful way to treat subordinates that does not belittle them in order to feed one's own ego. Leave that out of the workplace. Though such tactics may seem to work in the short-term, you will never get a successful workforce by bullying or devaluing your employees. You will most definitely burn them out, thus increasing the company's turn-over and the department's budget. The result will be an unnecessary waste of the company's money and time as it will require hiring and training new employees.

If you want to inspire your employees, you must learn to work with them in an efficient way that acknowledges and encourages their ambition. You have to let go of the old ways of doing things. Things like reinforcing chain of command and treating your staff like children should be left in the past. If an employee needs to be babysat, they probably shouldn't be working for you in the first place. After all, didn't you hire your employees so that you could free up your own time to focus on other issues? How does micromanaging them allow you to accomplish this? Just as people want to be treated as adults when they're not at work, they want that same respect in the workplace. Empowering your employees provides them with the opportunity to take on more owner-ship and responsibility, which translates into less issues for you to worry about. It's a win-win for everyone and it's a definite way that you can inspire and motivate your employees.

Another way to increase healthy competition in the workplace is by giving employees the opportunity to voice their ideas and acknowledge the value of their contributions. I used to work at a company where my boss took credit for my ideas and also those of the manager under me. My manager would voice his frustrations, and while I was happy he felt comfort able enough to confide in me, there was unfortunately nothing that I could do to help him. This killed me because I was his boss and I was supposed to support him. Because our supervisor was obsessed with power and the hierarchical structure in the work-place, we were only invited to certain meetings, thus eliminating any opportunity for us to voice our ideas. As a result, we had to turn in every creative concept that we came up with to our boss, and hope that he would somehow give us some credit for our efforts. We weren't asking for much—just the opportunity to own our hard work. Not long after that, my manager started looking for a new job. There was nothing I could do or say to convince him to stay. I watched his motivation slowly disappear. He was disheartened by the whole experience. It sucked all of the enjoyment and happiness from him that I witnessed when he first started. It was sad. So if you would like to continue to motivate your employees, let them feel the reward of having their voice.

Once again, just like sports, businesses have a certain amount of skill and talent, but what's the use of having those skills if you can't harness them and use them to your advantage? At my previous job there were many different departments who needed to communicate freely in order to be able produce the best product. Part of my job was to oversee tasks that would get passed along from one department to another, and it was my responsibility to ensure the task was completed by its designated deadline. One of the common themes I came across, was that many of the employees were frustrated and irritated by what they considered to be a lack of communication. Whether it was communication from one department to the other or from the top down, no one felt that the flow of information in the workplace was running smoothly. In fact, the common joke used to be that we had to decipher emails. More often than not my Senior Vice President would send me last-minute projects with minimal or no instructions or directions. Most of the time, I had absolutely no idea what she was talking about. Not only was I completely out of the loop, but I wasn't even aware the project she had given me existed. Had the company's corporate culture welcomed questions from its employees, I would have asked my SVP for some guidance. Since questions were not welcome, I made a habit of trying not to bother my superiors with any interruptions. Direction or no direction, the project was now on my plate, and it was up to me to try to figure it out.

This required a great deal of extra energy on every- one's part as the project not only affected me, but impacted other departments. It was my responsibility to find ways to inform each department of what was coming down the pike. I learned very quickly that in order to maximize time and get a project done as quickly as possible, it was best if I explained the task to all parties involved. Not only did this enable us to come together and act more like a team, but I learned that people are much more productive when they are invested in what they are working on. If a project is passed down without any context whatsoever, the motivation and effort are sacrificed. Think about it. You're more inclined to work hard on something when you know the role you are playing and feel as though you are contributing to a cause. The ability to see the bigger picture enhances the work. The more information you have, the better the job you can do.

When people within an organization are not communicating with one another properly, not only does it frustrate and annoy employees, but it creates resentment among departments and among the ranks. Animosity builds, and it ends up negatively affecting the work. People don't like to be blindsided, especially when a superior passes down a project that's been sitting on their desk and is now due ASAP. Obviously, there are always going to be fire drills and last-minute projects, but when it's an unnecessary emergency, time management needs to be addressed.

My experience in an extremely fast-paced working environment included projects that were frequently delegated at the last minute. Most of the time, these projects were just a part of the job, but every once in a while I'd get some mystery project handed to me at the final hour. The turnaround time was unrealistic, but in the end, a deadline is a deadline and I always met my deadlines. Had this been a common occurrence, it would have burned me out entirely. Not only would I have lost all motivation, but I'd have been too exhausted to get my job done well. When time is not managed appropriately in an organization, projects are more likely to slip through the cracks, deadlines are more likely to be missed, and work quality is definitely sacrificed. These are all negative outcomes, which would provide your company's competitors with a definite advantage.

In order to engage in healthy competition, a business must focus on itself. Once it has created a goal, it is now important for the business to find its market. Great companies listen to their customers. Having worked in marketing and advertising, I was able to see this first-hand. I used to market television shows. When we purchased media that selectively targeted a specific demographic, not only was it an efficient use of the budgeted advertising dollars, but it was also a successful and effective way to increase ratings. When the marketing for a television show was vague, our efforts were unsuccessful.

Great marketing and advertising strategies anticipate the consumer's wants and needs. They proactively seek the target audience and align themselves with entities that speak the same language as their audience. For example, when I worked in advertising I was working on the Western Lexus Dealer Association account. Lexus happened to be re-launching the IS, and it was my job to find and recommend creative ways for Lexus to reach its consumers. Due to the fact that the car targeted a younger demographic than the other Lexus car models, I needed to find ways to effectively reach this audience. Podcasting had just come on the scene, and there was an NPR station that spoke to a younger skewing audience. No one had used podcasting at that time to advertise, so the efficiency of the medium was not quantifiable. While aligning Lexus with the NPR station was a no-brainer, recommending that Lexus use podcasting as a means to get their message out there was a risk. It was a risk that I was willing to take. I presented my proposal to the Los Angeles Dealers and they immediately agreed to sign off on the deal. That initiative received national acclaim as it was written up in *WIRED Magazine, Ad Age* and *Ad Week.*

The reason my podcasting recommendation received such positive praise and exposure was because it was a seamless way to effectively target Lexus' IS audience in a completely uncluttered environment. It was a creative way to reach that demographic because it showed that we had been paying attention to their behavior.

If you look at places like Starbucks and Whole Foods, you will see the same thing. While their approach may be different, Starbucks and Whole Foods are great examples of companies that listen and pay attention to their consumers. These companies believe in continuous quality improvement. Instead of waiting for their competitors to catch up to them, they are constantly looking for ways to improve. How many times have you walked into a Starbucks or a Whole Foods and had that feeling that something was a little different and you kind of liked it? That's because Starbucks and Whole Foods anticipate their consumers' needs. Starbucks will often launch new products at specific locations to "test" them out, and Whole Foods will often rearrange their stores based on how their consumers shop and which departments are most popular. These are examples of businesses using competition and innovation to truly engage their audience.

Healthy competition among businesses enables them to better market themselves to the public by creating a dialogue with the consumer. Healthy competition in business makes businesses successful by building and establishing relationships with their audience. It creates an emotional connection. Take Nike for example. When I was a little girl, I remember seeing a magazine ad Nike had created that showed a woman running. It featured copy that spoke to the woman's sense of power when her feet hit the pavement and the strength she felt when she was giving it her all. It was the first ad that I can remember tearing out of a magazine and taping to my bedroom wall. That ad moved me. It was the first time I had ever seen anything from the media that actually spoke to the female athlete in me. The ad's copy enabled me to identify with the feelings of the woman running. I had those exact same feelings when I was swimming. The ad inspired me. Nike was now on my radar. Not only was it a brand that I was paying attention to, but it was a brand that somehow knew me. Nike, you see, had done a great job of connecting with the consumer. It elicited an emotional response.

Healthy competition in business is powerful. It creates products that never existed before. It challenges businesses to do their best, be their best. It screams, "Be as creative as possible, do anything you can imagine, create, innovate, build!" Healthy competition challenges businesses to do better, be better, and does not require the failure of your competitor in order for you to excel.

Competition Among Friends

The essence of competition is people trying to do their best so that they can "win". While we already know this and have talked about it, what we haven't talked about is how competitive we can be with our friends. It doesn't matter what the setting is, everyone's competitive. People are obsessed with winning.

While I'm sure every one of us has our own story to tell, most of us have fallen victim to an incident involving unhealthy competition. Isn't that sad? Why must this be the case? First, let's forgive ourselves. We're only human. We've been engaging in competitive behavior for as long as we can remember. From the time we were introduced to social groups, we were exposed to the concept of popularity. Popularity is merely the result of people competing with one another to be the most liked, the most well-known, the best athlete, the prettiest, the coolest and so on. While we may not be consciously engaging in this activity, our social institutions perpetuate this behavior.

I'm going to assume that you are familiar with the movie *Bridesmaids*. If you're not, I'll give you a brief recap. *Bridesmaids* is a story about two women who have just met. Both are friends of the bride, and they are competing to be the bride's best friend and maid of honor. The movie pokes fun at how ruthless women can be when vying for the same friend's attention. We laugh at the movie because we know there is some truth to it. Another example of competition among friends is the movie *Mean Girls*. Three of the most popular girls in high school take a new girl under their wing. It isn't long before that new girl begins to see just how fake popularity can be. The whole movie is about competition. It shows how the girls are competing for loyalty from their friends, adoration from their peers and attention from a guy.

Why do we have to cut one another down to size? Why must our competitor be less attractive, less wealthy and less talented for us to feel better about ourselves? Why can't we just see one another as different and appreciate those differences? Why must we engage in competition at the expense of another? Facebook and other forms of social media are a haven for this type of behavior. Who hasn't gone trolling on social media for an ex's new fling only to obsessively compare yourself to them? I don't know about you, but every time I engaged in that kind of behavior, I felt worse afterward. In fact, anytime I have gone on social media and compared other people's profiles and lives to mine, I always log off feeling slightly depressed. There have actually been studies on this that can back up my sentiments. Despite these awful feelings, we still continue to torture ourselves by logging on. Our curiosity gets the best of us, and then our egos kick in, and it's all downhill from there. This is unhealthy competition.

My suggestion is that when this happens, the best thing to do is log off, shut your computer and promise yourself that you will not play into this vicious viral behavior. I say vicious because what you're doing to yourself is vicious; it's actually torture. Your competitive nature is seeking the power in this imaginary relationship and the worst part is, you're never going to get it. The only way to win this competition and truly get the power back is to redirect your energy, focus on yourself and not care. It's not easy, but I can promise you that from personal experience, it does get easier in time. You begin to see how much happier you are when you're not engaging in negative competition and realize how truly toxic that behavior is. This, of course, takes mindfulness and the ability to be conscious of your actions. Once we become aware of our behavior and how our actions make us feel, we can change them to be more beneficial and positive.

I was watching *Chopped*, this amazing cooking competition show on the Food Network, and witnessed two professional, well-known chefs engage in healthy competition. These chefs were so secure in their own abilities that they were supportive and friendly. They were laughing and having fun while running around the kitchen. Watching it made me smile. These chefs respected each other's talents and skills in the kitchen and knew that their competitor's ability to concoct creative dishes did not diminish their own efforts. In fact, it was the opposite. Knowing that their competitor was talented, encouraged them to challenge themselves. It resulted in better dishes because each chef was inspired by the other. Each chef was able to accept constructive criticism from the judges without having to tear down the other competitor. There have been times when I've watched *Chopped* and the competitors have been ruthless. They were throwing one another under the bus and insulting each other in front of the judges while being critiqued. It made my stomach churn and left a bad taste in my mouth. It made me uncomfortable in my own living room. I was embarrassed for them and by them.

When we're secure and comfortable with our competitiveness, we don't feel threatened by our friends or our competitors. It is when our jealousy and insecurities arise from unhealthy competitiveness that negative circumstances present themselves.

Having had a few too many unhealthy competitive interactions, I've since learned how to detect the warning signs and see when the issue is with me or other people. It would be ideal if this behavior did not exist. Unfortunately, since it does, we have to learn how to decode our behavior and turn an unhealthy competitive situation into a positive one. We do not have to change the other person. All we have to do is focus on ourselves. The dynamic is what it is. You can't do anything about it. I've spent years trying to play other people's games, and all it has done is wasted a lot of my time and energy. It's not worth it. What I should have done was ignore the other person. Their feelings were their responsibility, not mine; I had a choice not to engage. As long as you learn how not to feed these negative behaviors, you can learn how to survive. I say survive because when people engage in unhealthy competitive behavior, things can get nasty and they can monopolize your life. If I want to waste my time and energy, at least let me decide how I'm going to do it, and even if I want to "play the game".

In life, there are activities that do have rules that require learning a specific skill, which set goals, provide you with feedback, and make control possible. Unfortunately, hanging out with friends is not one of them. Due to this fact, it is incumbent on you to create your own experiences so that when you are faced with unhealthy competition, you will be better able to navigate these situations.

Suppressing Your Competitive Spirit

Most of us feel uncomfortable when faced with our competitive nature. As I mentioned earlier, I certainly did. Competitive feelings do not play favorites. You can feel competitive toward anyone—family members, friends, coworkers, even strangers. Since our competitive feelings are unacceptable to us, we disregard them and shrug them off, labeling them as nothing to be concerned about; thus we do not deal with them. Rather than disintegrating into thin air, like we wish most feelings we dismiss would do, they sit with us, taunting us until they manage to unleash themselves in a way we had never intended them to.

Suppressing your competitive nature prevents you from being able to express yourself freely. It does not allow you to own your feelings, so instead they sit with you until you do. There was a certain guy who used to train with me. He would always "be on me" in practice. For those that are unfamiliar with this term, it means that as we swam laps, he was drafting off me and using my momentum to give him more speed. He would shorten his breaks in between sets so he could push off the wall sooner to be closer behind me. It drove me crazy. However, I did not confront him. Why? Like it or not, I was not being honest with myself and acknowledging my competitive feelings. I secretly wanted to be so much faster than him that even if he pushed off the wall immediately behind me, he would never catch me. I was playing his game and I had no idea.

When competitiveness is not dealt with, it can lead to anger, resentment, and disappointment—all feelings that are emotionally exhausting. It's no wonder I swam slower when I focused on my competitors. I was so caught up in being annoyed and angry, that I had little energy left for practice.

Another example of ignoring your competitive nature is secretly wishing someone else to be less than you. On my California club swim team, there was a girl who would always try to compete with me. She would do it in practice, but especially in meets. In fact, this was the same girl whose mother used to stand behind my lane and time me. She and her mom were so competitive that they would track my times and write them down. I was faster than her in every stroke, and

I guess our times were close in some events, but it was only their crazy behavior that got my attention. As we got older, I let the situation get the best of me. She surpassed me in the freestyle events. I held on to my butterfly, breaststroke and 400 IM. I most certainly was not going to let her have those events too. When she did catch up to me, I got jealous. It wasn't harmless jealousy either. I would give her the evil stare down when she wasn't looking and make sure I was always far away from her, even when she was being friendly to me. I completely disassociated myself from her and would barely acknowledge her when she would speak to me. Was that normal? No. Am I proud of my behavior? Absolutely not. I was jealous, and jealousy makes you do things you later look back on and cringe. It brings out the worst in people. What we need to learn to do when these feelings arise is deal with them and not ignore them.

Suppressing our competitive nature can also make us cynical. We stop trying as hard and tend to steer away from the things that are making us feel this way when we should be addressing them. Take that girl I was just talking about. When she started beating me, I literally stopped swimming some events. I began thinking that I was not good enough, or that the event was not the best suited for me. I told myself that I was a distance swimmer and that the event was too short, which meant I wouldn't really start getting into my groove until the race was almost over. While some of this may have been true, that's not the point. The point is that my negative attitude, my cynicism, was getting the best of me, and it was preventing me from being able to perform. It took away my competitive advantage completely by overshadowing it with doom and gloom. I would turn into Eeyore from Winnie the Pooh.

If you think about other behaviors that occur when we're being competitive, gossiping comes to mind. Gossiping can make you feel better about yourself. There is a false justification for your feelings when others are in agreement with you. While the pickup may be brief, feeding off another's misery is a sick drug, but some of us enjoy taking it.

When gossiping is taken to the extreme it can result in bullying, another form of unhealthy competition. Bullies are not in touch with their competitive feelings. They feel threatened by others and their way of dealing with these emotions is to attack people in order to enhance their own self-esteem. A bully doesn't think they're engaging in competition at all, which is why it is a prime example of an individual suppressing their competitive nature. They often choose to pick on people who they perceive to be weaker or more vulnerable. The fact is that these bullies suffer from their own insecurities. Having been bullied in elementary school, I learned at a very young age the kind of person I never wanted to be. I also knew that I never wanted to make anyone feel even remotely close to the way I was made to feel, even if it was my enemy. If I were to engage in that type of behavior, gossiping and bullying someone else simply because I was insecure and felt threatened, I know that it would get me nowhere. I'd still have to live with my uncomfortable competitive feelings.

What causes someone to feel threatened? Competition. People who mean nothing to us are not even on our radar. You ignore them. You only notice someone if they are relevant to you or you make them relevant. It is the individuals who catch our attention that we find ourselves preoccupied with and comparing ourselves to. That is why the opposite of love is not hate, but indifference.

Owning your competitive nature is kind of like being asked to describe yourself and being told that you must include your negative attributes as well as your positive ones. You're already stressing, because who wants to admit their faults? Who wants to deal with the negative? You're perfect, right? You have no negatives. Wrong. You know only too well what your negatives are; you just don't want to vocalize them. Vocalizing them would be admitting they're real, and you want to be known for your positive attributes only. This simply is not possible. You need the yin to have the yang.

Competition can be ambiguous, misconstrued and misjudged. Healthy competition doesn't have to be. When we learn to acknowledge our emotions, both the good and the bad, we free ourselves. Then we have nothing to hide, nothing to be afraid of, and nothing a friend or enemy can say that will hurt us because everything's already out there. We've already owned up to who we are.

It is possible that our competitiveness can turn on us, creating an extremely unhealthy internal struggle. How many of us are our own worst enemy? I don't know about you, but if this were a classroom, I'd be raising both hands. I say things to myself that I would never say to anyone. Why? I'm being competitive. With whom? Myself. I've looked around and seen the people I admire, the people I respect, the ones who have achieved great things and I start comparing myself to them. I start feeling incapable, lackluster, eh. My negativity has gotten me to quit before I've even started. I remove myself from the game before the game begins because I'm too afraid to fail. Remember the female swimmer who became faster than I was in freestyle? Since I was so convinced I was going to fail or not succeed the way I wanted to— which is my definition of failure—I automatically thought, *it's not worth it*. The problem is, though, all I could do is think about the missed opportunity and wonder. This is what I mean when I say that being honest with your competitive nature allows you to dream and shows you what you value. By ignoring those feelings, they don't all of a sudden stop. You don't stop wanting what you want. You still dream your dream, but the dream gets dimmer and the passion less persistent.

I unfortunately had to learn this the hard way. At some swim meets, I was so good at psyching myself out that all of my energy was spent on trying to manage my internal struggle. That is probably why my mom could tell how I was going to do in my race just from looking at my stance on the starting block. Isn't it amazing what our minds can do? They can be our best friend or our worst enemy. I guess the decision is up to you. I choose best friend.

Competition and Doubt

*M*errriam *Webster's Dictionary* defines *doubt* as "to have uncertainty, to believe that something may not be true or is unlikely, to have no confidence in something or someone."

I hate doubt. I have thoughts of doubt I try to control. Sometimes it creeps up on me when I'm watching TV or reading something that relates to a goal of mine. I'll start feeling an insane amount of anxiety. My mind will start racing, and I can feel my heart beating faster. I've actually had to stop watching certain TV shows as a result. Sounds crazy, right? Whatever I'm doing to myself creates such an intense reaction that it affects me physically.

I've been doing a lot of work on myself and have really been trying to understand my thoughts and my behavior, so I've had time to analyze the unanticipated reaction that I just mentioned. What I realized about my emotions was that the intense response I was having was due to doubt. I had been comparing myself to the people featured on TV. Being an ambitious woman who wants to be successful, I was watching a segment on women who have significantly impacted their industry, leading to changes in our culture. At first I was excited to learn about these women. But as the documentary progressed, there came a point where my subconscious connected with my conscious and I became consumed with negative feelings. These negative feelings caused me to doubt myself as I began to think, "Oh my goodness, I'm never going to be able to do that; look at how young that woman was when she accomplished that. I'm already older than that now, so maybe my time has passed? I'll never be as successful as I want to be." I was completely overwhelmed and deflated. I got that feeling of having so much to accomplish in a limited amount of time that I had absolutely no idea where to even start. I felt lost.

All of the emotions I have described above are feelings of doubt. They are the result of an inner monologue we create that tells us we can't do something. Sometimes it acts as a voice-over telling me, "I can't. It won't happen. I have so far to go. It's going to take too long. Does anybody believe in me? Everyone thinks I'm foolish for wanting or dreaming of this. It's not attainable" and on and on and on. The mind never stops, especially if you let it continue on like that.

The reason for the doubt I have described above is due to competition. Yup, competition. You see, we are creatures of habit, and since childhood, one of our habits has been to compare ourselves to others. Whether we're comparing our looks, our athletic ability, or our intellect, it doesn't matter. The point is that we spend a majority of our conscious and subconscious time competing with others. Kind of makes you stop and think, right? Right about now you're probably wondering if what I've said above is true and if so, does it relate to you? Are you engaging in this behavior without even being aware of it? If you are, it's fine. It doesn't mean that something is wrong with you. I'm just making a point by making you aware of how prevalent competition is in our society, our culture, our corporations and our interpersonal interactions. This is why understanding doubt is so important.

The worst case of doubt that I can remember was at the Junior Olympics. It was the same Junior Olympics where I won the 200 meter breaststroke. I was having a phenomenal meet. I was shedding seconds off my times. It was awesome. What was not awesome, however, was my 400 IM race. I was swimming the 400 IM in finals and I was stoked. I don't remember what number seed I was, but if I had to guess I'd say it was anywhere from third to fifth place. I was excited. When the race began, I started out strong. I was always a good butterflier so I wasn't worried about that. What I was worried about was my backstroke. That was my least favorite stroke, and it was also my weakest. See the correlation? I was swimming my last lap of backstroke when I took a quick peek at my competition and my current standing. I was in second or third place. I actually might have been in first place at that moment. It wasn't until I freaked out and choked that I lost my competitive edge and my standing. Somewhere in those few seconds I let my mind create all of this doubt. I even remember thinking (and this is embarrassing for me to admit) that I didn't deserve to be winning. I didn't deserve to be going as fast as I was. I remember doubting myself to the point where I questioned my skills and my ability to swim fast, thinking that my stellar performance wasn't supposed to happen. How crazy is that? To this day, I still have moments where I wonder what would have happened had I not lost focus.

So, how do you pull yourself out of doubt once it creeps up on you? I have now learned to better manage my thoughts. One of the first things my therapist told me during one of our sessions, was that there is good news and bad news. The good news is that I'm a conceptual thinker. The bad news is that I am going to have to learn how to control my thoughts. I looked at her in confusion, and just before my mind began to respond to what she had just said and run off in a negative direction, she said, "It's not a bad thing. Just something to be aware of." Of course, still being the curious person I am and needing to have all the answers, I said, "I shouldn't see it like a chore? See it as a good thing, an opportunity?" She said, "Yes, exactly." So I let the negative thoughts that were about to fill my mind dissipate and I solely kept that one line in my head. "You're going to have to learn how to control your thoughts." Rather than judge or label them, I had to learn just to observe them.

Controlling your thoughts is imperative to achieving your goals. It is a key strategy I've used to help me battle my doubts. I've also learned to do things like take a time out. So if, for example, I'm looking at someone's tricked out, amazing website, comparing it to mine and starting to feel less than, I stop and become aware of what's happening by analyzing my emotions. I then go back and ask myself why am I feeling the way I am. I replay the answers in my head and decode my negative thoughts. After that, I close my computer, take my dog for a walk, watch TV, eat a snack—anything that will take my mind off comparing my website to the other person's. I do this because at that point in time, as soon as that negativity and doubt arose, my task no longer became productive. I was no longer capable of being 100% present. How could I be, if most of my energy was being spent comparing myself to someone else, and then judging myself poorly as a result?

Another way I've learned to deal with my doubts has been to talk about them with someone. Not only has this helped get me out of my own head, but it's provided me with a different perspective. Being able to look at things differently is beyond helpful when these situations occur. Otherwise, if you're anything like me, your thoughts will just sit with you and build upon one another until you feel so uncertain, insecure and anxiety-ridden that giving up will seem like the only answer. Should you make this mistake, which I have made many times, and let your thoughts get the best of you, try not to make any rash decisions until you've cooled off. I'm an emotional person, so when my thoughts get out of control in a not-so-healthy way, I've had to learn that acting on impulse is not the best thing. Too many times have I acted irrationally and worked myself up, only to exert all of this unnecessary energy. I'd rather keep anyone else from having to waste time making that same mistake. If you do, forgive yourself, or try to. It happens. Look at it as a learning experience for next time.

Our thoughts can be so powerful that as you can see, they can control our emotions and even our actions. They do this without us even realizing it, because it all happens so fast. Recognizing the patterns will help keep doubt at bay, and in turn motivate you so that you can and will achieve your dreams.

Competition and Fear

A more extreme type of doubt is fear. Fear can be debilitating. It can prevent us from living our lives. It can keep us from even thinking about what we want because we're too afraid of what might happen if we want it. Fear lives in a world of "what ifs" that are not dependent on reality. There are times, however, when fear can be used to your advantage and can even be exhilarating.

While I was in college, I spent the second semester of my junior year studying abroad. The program was called Semester at Sea. When I signed up for Semester at Sea I had zero idea of what the experience was going to be. I suppose it was good that I had no expectations, but I could not have gone into that experience less informed than I was. I'm serious. I was so uninformed that my mom basically packed my bags. After all, she had read the material, so she knew what I needed much more than I did. I just knew that I wanted to bring a camera. My dad loaned me his. I also knew that I wanted to bring some journals. I always loved writing and what better way to document a trip like this than writing about it. I signed up for a room with a porthole, and I was going to be placed with a roommate I had never met before. The ship had no internet, and it was about $10 a minute to call home. I was taking a big risk.

I met up with a friend in Colorado and stayed there for a few days, and then we left for the Bahamas. The ship was departing from Nassau. I'll never forget that day. It was an experience I do not wish to relive. I kept saying to myself, "What are you doing here?" I was so unprepared that I had absolutely no idea what to expect. I think I might have researched my room so that I could see what it looked like. After what felt like hours waiting in line boarding and going through customs, I finally stood outside my room. I put my luggage down and I turned the key. When I saw the tiny space where I would be spending the next few months, the first thing I did was drop to my knees and cry. I was scared. This was fear. I was already on the boat. There was no escape. Looking back, I'm glad I was stuck on that boat. It was one of the best experiences of my life. What I've realized years later is how many fears I conquered while traveling abroad without even knowing it. It was a life-changing experience.

I was reading an interesting article the other day that talked about the combination of fun and fear. The article was about a woman who was in love with surfing. She spoke about how she hated high school and turned to surfing for her sanity. She said that until she started surfing, she did not know how pleasurable fear could be. It wasn't necessarily the fear, but the desire to conquer it and the thrill she got from doing just that. In her eyes, adult life can be filled with things that we fear, but that fear can create invigorating experiences that keep us coming back. Fear is a vital response to physical and emotional danger. When we challenge ourselves beyond our limits, there is always the fear of the unknown.

One of my experiences confronting fear occurred when I was getting ready to swim finals in the 200 meter breaststroke. I had two hours before my race to go home and rest. I was afraid this down-time was going to be a struggle for me. Two hours to get in my head. No, thank you. Fortunately, I was able to keep my fear at bay and actually use it as an asset. I was able to feed off my anxiety and turn it into excitement and energy.

As I stood behind those blocks before my race, I remember the sun was going down. There was a coolness in the air. I got goose-bumps. This was my moment. This was everything I had worked for. The official said, "Take your mark," and as soon as I heard the beep, my heart dropped into my stomach. You obviously already know the end to this story. I was able to conquer my fear and use it to my competitive advantage. That is exactly what fear can do in competition. It can become your greatest asset, your secret weapon.

Competition and Anger

Anger is emotionally exhausting. It literally sucks up all of your energy. Did you know that anger is a secondary emotion? You physically have to feel another emotion before you get angry. Anger and competition often go hand in hand. How many rivalries do you know that involve trash talking? These people aren't smiling and happy when they're tearing each other down—they're angry.

Whenever I got angry, I swam my worst. I lost my ability to focus. With my head no longer in the game, how could I expect to perform at my own elite level? On the other hand, when it came to relays, I was at my happiest. I always had the most fun and swam my best. I would be laughing and joking around behind the starting block, up until it was my time to swim. My times reflected my attitude. When I was happy, I was swimming fast. When I was angry, I was fighting the water, not moving with it. I actually talked a little about this earlier when I mentioned that guy who used to "be on me" in practice. That's a perfect example of someone making me angry.

I laugh now when I think about it, but back then it made me clench my fists and grind my teeth. Well, remember how I said that I wished I could have been faster than him? What do you think was the reason this was not possible? I was too busy being angry.

Another example of anger getting in my way was when I would let my competitor's behavior rattle me. The girl whose mom used to stand behind my lane and time me made me angry. When you're angry you become obsessed. All of your attention is on the actions of your opponent, and you're fixated on the situation that made you angry to begin with. You're not focusing on what needs to be done for you to perform your best. It's like a dog chasing its tail—you go nowhere.

So how does one refrain from getting angry so that it doesn't mess with your ability to compete? When I learned that anger is a secondary emotion, I used that to my advantage. The way I see it, I have to be feeling something first. It's up to me to identify what that emotion is. I also know that, for the most part, my anger is a reaction to my wanting to control a situation that I cannot control. Knowing these two things helps me identify my thoughts so that I can unravel my feelings. I say unravel because anger gets you all tied up in knots. You're not thinking straight, your heart is racing, and your face feels flushed. It's hard to stop the anger train once you get it started if you don't know how. I guess you could let it play out, but if you're trying to save time and energy, I recommend dissecting your thoughts instead.

After all the craziness has subsided and you've successfully managed to subdue your anger, you're most likely going to come up with the right words that can help you express your emotions. That's what happens to me. I find myself getting these epiphanies; I can finally put my finger on what exactly upset me.

Lately, my emotional reaction to anger has shifted completely. As opposed to getting upset and all bent out of shape, I get motivated. Who would have thought? It's actually kind of awesome. I acknowledge whatever is making me angry, and I fling it aside. Half the time I laugh when I do this because I realize how ridiculous it is. I must say, this new approach is quite refreshing. To be clear, I'm talking about the kind of anger that comes from life's annoyances—all of the unhealthy negative behaviors that confront us every day. They are all nuisances that take up energy we do not wish to give. This is why I'm happy to report that now my anger motivates me in a positive way. It fuels my engine and fills my tank.

While I'd rather anger not be my main form of motivation, I'll take it. Some people perform their best when motivated by anger. They're able to channel that energy and use it to their competitive advantage. Rather than let that anger hold them back, they own it and work through it. Anger gains its power when you're not seeking redemption or revenge. There's no "I told you so." It's more of a thought mixed with a feeling. The thought says, "Ok, you think that of me? Huh…interesting. Alright." Then you sit in silence with that information for a brief moment. The thought is simply observed, not judged, analyzed or dissected, just observed. Then you kind of smirk and smile as you're reminded of your goal. You know without a doubt that no one can take your goal away from you, least of all with their silly words, thoughts or feelings. You find yourself feeling inspired, driven. A sense of power comes over you.

When I was in high school I would have horrible days, as most teenagers do. I'd find out that my crush didn't like me and was interested in dating my friend. I'd get into a fight with a girlfriend of mine. A teacher would embarrass me in class. These situations all felt dramatic and life-threatening because I was in high school. Everything feels much worse when you're that age. None of it was really all that horrible. It just felt like my life was over. By the end of the day I had no fight left in me. Waiting for my ride to swim practice, I wondered how my mood would affect my workout. By the time I jumped into the pool, my body and my head felt lighter. Eventually, I'd notice that my headache was gone and that my body was warm as I started sweating from the workout. As I got older, I began to realize what was happening. When I was in the pool, I was home. It was my temple, and no one was going to take that away from me. No matter how bad a day I had I always knew that I had swimming, and that was all I needed to keep me sane. No one was going to take away my sense of self and tell me who I was or what I was capable of. I was in charge. The dramatic distractions of my school day weren't welcome. In fact, they didn't even exist. The negativity from others tries to push you off your feet and make you lose your balance, but like one of those inflatable rocking dolls that never fall down, you too stand your ground, unfazed and unaffected by it all. It's a wonderfully liberating feeling when you realize that the only person that can take you down is yourself.

Competition and Social Media

Social media is a hot-button issue these days. Much of the controversy is due to the fact that something that is supposed to connect us and enable better communication frequently leads to jealousy, misunderstanding and drama. Social media has given birth to a competitive environment that now merges our online and offline lives. Invading our personal space, the line between these two worlds is often blurred. It took me a long time to make friends with the concept of social media. This is odd behavior for me too, as I consider myself to be an early adopter. I guess I just don't feel the need to put myself in what I consider to be an unhealthy competitive environment. Why is it unhealthy? Because we make it that way.

How many times have you logged onto Facebook and felt worse than you did before you logged on? For me, I would say that it is often. People use Facebook as a personal marketing tool. They use it to promote themselves and the life they want others to think they have. They engage in this unhealthy competition where they compete for the best "life" and the judge of that "life" is how tricked out their profile is. How many vacation pictures do they have? How many family pictures, pictures of their children, their friends, and their moments of having fun can they post? Does all of this information need to be shared? Absolutely not. I am not the best person to answer that question, however, as I'm much more private than most people and feel very strongly about my privacy. The way I see it, you're on a need-to-know basis. If I don't think the information is any of your business, you do not need to know.

The reason I'm not the biggest fan of social media is that I feel like it can bring out the absolute worst in people. While I'm all for the first amendment and having the means for sharing special moments with others, I think we've taken it a little too far. We don't all need to know what everyone is doing, where they are, what they're thinking, what they're eating, how they're feeling and their unsolicited opinion on every issue. No offense, but not many of us actually care. I'd much rather catch up with someone in person to find out how they are doing and what they have been up to. I'm not the best at keeping in touch with friends who live elsewhere, so social media helps in those instances. It's great to see that old friends who I haven't connected with in a long time are happy and are doing well. I love that. I don't, however, find myself using Facebook's messaging as my default. For whatever reason, I prefer to take our conversations off of social media. In my opinion, doing so makes these communications feel more intimate and special.

I do think that social media provides people with great outlets where they can express their creativity, such as YouTube. But even that can be ruined when people feel the need to write nasty and hateful comments on people's pages. How disheartening! I do not see the point of internet trolls. Yes, your opinion matters, but do you really need to make someone else feel awful to make yourself feel better? How insecure are you? Remember when we talked about bullies and what happens to people when they suppress their competitive nature? Case in point. If social media fostered a healthier competitive environment in which people were inspired by one another as opposed to being threatened, I'd be much more of a supporter. In the meantime, not so much.

I used to work in the advertising industry and am currently in the business of marketing. So how is it possible for a marketing person to be anti-social media? Well, for starters, I am not anti-social media. I say to each their own. I give social media props for employing the most effective and simplistic way of marketing, word of mouth. Social media forums capitalize on this very notion by helping people spread the word, regardless of whether the word is good or bad. One problem I see with social media as it relates to business, is that companies who market or advertise in the social media space cannot expect to change, alter or control an environment that's predicated upon unpredictable organic human behavior. Now, while I've definitely had successful experiences marketing products on social media, I would say that the most successful campaigns were the ones that created partnerships with social media sites to do something that had not been done before. Social media was used in conjunction with other marketing tactics, so that the two could support one another and reinforce the message to the designated target audience. An example of this would be promoting new video content on high profile online sites and using that video content to engage the consumer and ultimately drive them to visit a specific page on Facebook.

Being more connected has its perks, but it has also changed the way that we communicate. No longer satisfied with our conversations, we analyze the rate at which they occur. One time my girlfriend and I both sent a text message to a friend of ours. When I was the first to receive a response, my girlfriend's feelings were hurt. She wondered why she never heard back from our friend. Faced with a new kind of uncomfortable situation, I reassured my girlfriend that the lack of response meant nothing. Our friend probably figured that we were both hanging out together and decided to respond to the both of us with one simple text. I just happened to be the one to receive it. While this subtle competition existed prior to social media, the difference now is that we can unfortunately see our communications in real time. We post, tag and tweet, hoping for the support from our friends as we place a value on ourselves based on the number of comments we receive and on how quickly we receive them. As a result, we've all become addicted to instant validation and gratification. We expect others to drop everything and get back to us right away because we know they've received our message. We can see it.

How can we create a healthy competitive environment in the online space on sites like YouTube, Facebook, Twitter and LinkedIn where the number of views, likes, posts, followers and connections tend to dictate your sense of worth? Short answer, don't buy into it. I'm not saying you shouldn't engage in social media. I'm saying you shouldn't let yourself get caught up in the hype.

Don't let your sense of self and your self-esteem be determined by the profiles you see online. People need to feel connected, and in my opinion, that connection happens much more organically in person. That's why people who are speaking to one another online to see if there's a romantic connection eventually meet in person. They want to see if there's a spark, chemistry and a level of comfort with one another. This is not something that they can conclude by communicating online.

We also need to do a better job of connecting with ourselves and knowing our sense of worth as opposed to letting others tell us what it is. When you learn to love yourself and compete in a healthy manner, you realize that all of the stuff that irritates you when you log on is part of a game, and it's a game you should make a conscious effort not to play. Why? Because it is unhealthy and unproductive. Why engage in unhealthy behavior when you have a choice? No one is making you fall victim to unhealthy competition that forces you to ramp up your social media profile to the point that it doesn't even describe the life you're truly leading. While I understand the need to put on a good face and focus on the positive things in your life, ask yourself, is this what I'm really doing? If it is, great. I do know, however, that I'm not the only one who sees the phoniness in the unforgivably competitive social media environment.

Many of my friends have confided in me, telling me how they felt worse after having logged on and looked at the profile of so-and-so. I have friends who have broken up with boyfriends, ended relationships with their friends, resigned from jobs and divorced their husbands, and now they absolutely refuse to log on for fear of having to relive it all. What these friends are referring to is the vicious unhealthy competitive cycle we call social media. It wouldn't be so vicious if it didn't make us all feel so bad.

I started noticing which supposed "friends" made me feel uneasy when I logged on and I deleted them. I no longer felt the desire nor the need to engage in any unhealthy competitive behavior I did not absolutely have to. It was my choice. I bring this up as a possible solution on how to create a healthier competitive atmosphere within your social media environment. Remember, not all competition is unhealthy. When your friends inspire and challenge you, they are having a positive influence on your life and you're grateful for it. That is exactly the type of healthy competition I'm talking about and that I'd like to see more of in the social media arena. Wouldn't that be nice?

Competition and Motivation

Motivation can spring from a variety of feelings. It can also occur when you least expect it. In fact, did you know that envy can be used to motivate you? Remember how we talked about not suppressing your competitive nature? Don't sit with negative emotions, but instead let them motivate you to do something positive for yourself.

When motivation occurs, dopamine is released in the brain. I read a study in which research showed spikes in dopamine in individuals during moments of high stress. Considering moments of high stress cannot by any stretch of the imagination be considered pleasurable—unless you're a masochist of course—it was concluded that dopamine didn't just relate to pleasure. Dopamine's true effect may in fact be motivation. Apparently dopamine performs its task before we obtain our rewards. Therefore, its real job is to take action and motivate us to do something. There was a behavioral neuroscientist I was reading about who confirmed that there was a link between motivation and dopamine when he performed a study on rats. In the study, rats were given two choices of food, one easily accessible pile of food or another larger pile of food that was behind a small fence. He observed that the rats with lower levels of dopamine almost always took the easy way out, choosing the smaller pile of food instead of the larger one behind the fence. The study revealed that animals with low levels of dopamine were less likely to work for things. This conclusion demonstrated dopamine's role as it relates to motivation.

While fascinating, the study's results are not surprising. What do you feel when a wave of motivation comes over you? High. This is why you see some athletes struggle with retirement. They've spent their entire life challenging themselves, keeping motivated so that they can perform at an elite level. They've felt the lows, but more importantly they lived through and thrived on the highs. Why do you think they continued doing what they were doing? It felt good. Not only did winning feel good, but achieving their goals did too, and there's no way they could have achieved their goals had they not found a way to keep themselves motivated. To be expected to all of a sudden give that up is not only difficult, it's heartbreaking. For so long you've identified yourself as one kind of person, but now your time's up and you're expected to find a new identity and let go of the past.

When I quit swimming, I lost a large part of myself. While it was my decision to walk away, I had absolutely no idea that by doing so, my sense of self would be deeply affected as well. I mean, who was I if I was no longer a swimmer? How could I center myself if I did not have my temple anymore? How could I stay as strong as I used to feel both physically and mentally?

It took some time for me to learn how to become whole again after I quit swimming. It was not an easy transition, but I had to adapt. Continuing to swim for fun on my own saved me as I didn't completely leave my sanctuary. My lifestyle, my body and my mind, however, felt drastically different than it did when I was training and competing. I think that is why I am able to identify with athletes who talk about the hardships they encounter when they retire; when the source of the motivation they once thrived on is now gone and has to be replaced. Keeping motivated, you see, is an art of sorts. When you've spent most of your life relying on your peak performances and career highlights to motivate you, how can anyone expect it to be painless when what inspired all of your success and self-worth no longer exists?

This is why learning how stay motivated is much more difficult than it looks. While it may be easy when you're traveling down one road, what happens when the road splits and you're forced to choose another path? Just like Robert Frost's poem, "The Road Not Taken."

The Road Not Taken
By Robert Frost

Two roads diverged in a yellow wood,
And sorry I could not travel both
And be one traveler, long I stood
And looked down one as far as I could
To where it bent in the undergrowth;
Then took the other, as just as fair,
And having perhaps the better claim,
Because it was grassy and wanted wear;
Though as for that the passing there
Had worn them really about the same,
And both that morning equally lay
In leaves no step had trodden black.
Oh, I kept the first for another day!
Yet knowing how way leads on to way,
I doubted if I should ever come back.
I shall be telling this with a sigh
Somewhere ages and ages hence:
Two roads diverged in a wood, and I—
I took the one less traveled by,
And that has made all the difference.

This poem is one of my favorites. It reminds me that, no matter which road I take, in the end I ultimately have the choice. I can choose to see my journey as a new challenge and an opportunity for a new adventure. As many of you know, sometimes in life the road that looks best is not the one you get to take. But the gratitude you find along the way allows you to look back and see the beauty in having taken the more difficult path. I once went on a date with this guy who told me he thought people who went through hard times had more personality. Having been through my own series of rough times, not only did I appreciate his perspective, but I found it enlightening and uplifting. That's how I feel about Robert Frost's poem.

After I stopped swimming competitively, I had to figure out what else motivated me—it was learning. When I was learning, I was inspired and I was passionate. I noticed that passion was a common theme. I had it when I swam, and now I had it when I was learning. It actually started me thinking. What was passion if not an incentive to challenge oneself? Didn't one have to be passionate in order to have a goal? Would you work toward achieving something if you weren't passionate about it? Motivation may not be one size fits all, yet passion is an underlying theme for those who achieve their goals. While passion may not feel the same to everyone, I can't think of a situation when someone is motivated and passion is absent. Perhaps the best way to be competitive is to find your passion button, press it, and take it from there.

Gaining a Competitive Advantage

After I won my race at Junior Olympics, I had a much different perspective on competition. I was able to see the difference between unhealthy and healthy competition. I was training for Junior Nationals in the 200 meter butterfly, when the thought of quitting first entered my mind. At first, I ignored the idea. I kept on swimming. I didn't want to be one of those swimmers I saw growing up who hit their peak, retired their dream, then traded in their swimsuit to sit in the stands and just watch. They were burned out or injured. I didn't want to be a statistic, a burnout. The thought alone killed me. Eventually, I had to come to terms with how I was feeling because the thought of quitting ended up affecting how I felt when I was training. I was no longer inspired.

My coach and my parents left the decision of quitting up to me. While I desperately wanted to know what they thought about my quitting, they refused to weigh in. I was annoyed at the time but also knew that they were right—I was the one who had to make that decision. I was only fifteen years old and I kept thinking about how competitive I wanted to be during high school swim season, and how crazy it would make me if my former opponents beat me. I knew that if I decided to walk away from competitive swimming, my fears would become a reality and that pained me.

In making the decision of whether to quit or not, I had to do some soul-searching. I began observing other athletes. I started watching different sports and documenting what I saw. What I began to notice were common themes that applied to all sports. I saw three things that must exist in order for me or any athlete to perform at their highest level. I started to develop a theory.

As this theory evolved, I saw that it didn't just apply to sports. It applied to any competitive situation. Looking back, it was almost as if I were conducting my own experiment without even knowing it and committing the results to memory. What can I say? I found human behavior fascinating, especially when it came to how people behaved when competing. In constructing my theory, I became aware of how the passion and desire I once felt for competitive swimming was not as strong as it had been. The answer to my decision became obvious. It was then that I quit swimming competitively. I wanted to love it, not resent it. That's why I began swimming in the first place. The thought of resenting something that I loved doing, was unacceptable. I didn't want to go out that way. I was going to write my own story. I wasn't going to sit in the stands. I was still going to swim, but this time it would be for pure joy, not for competition.

In order for a person to excel at something and be able to compete over and over again, three things have to exist. All three things have to be present with no exception. Those three things are Heart, Hunger and Hard Work. I call them the 3 H's. Time and time again as I watched competitive situations around me, I was able to see a significant, unquestionable difference in those that won and those that lost.

Let me begin by clarifying what it means to win and what it means to lose. You might think that that's obvious, but not so much. While I used this analogy earlier in this book, it's worth repeating. Winning is meeting your own expectations or exceeding them. You're setting your own goals and accomplishing them, and it means so much more to you than coming in first place. When I competed and I swam slower than I wanted to and still came in first place, was I happy? Sure. Was I satisfied? Absolutely not. When I was competing and I finished second or third and swam much faster than I had expected to, I was ecstatic. Yes it would have been nice to win, but I was more focused on my time than I was on my place. That is healthy competition.

Losing on the other hand, meant focusing on my teammate's mom standing behind my lane timing me, or trolling social media looking for my latest fling's new girlfriend just so that I could see what she looked like and make sure that she wasn't prettier. I call that losing because it's unhealthy competition. It's not bringing out the best in me. In fact it's doing the exact opposite. It's not making me more evolved as a person. There's no challenge for me to overcome. In both examples, I'm competing with something that is completely out of my control. I can't control my teammate's mom and I most certainly cannot wave a magic wand and make that girl less attractive. It's wasted energy and more importantly, it's unhealthy competition.

Unhealthy competition is the act of focusing on others rather than yourself and using unhealthy emotions in harmful ways. The irony is that these negative emotions end up hurting you more than your competitors. I'm guessing that's not what you're going for.

One surefire way to walk away from unhealthy competition and toward healthy competition is by using the 3 H's, Heart, Hunger and Hard Work. These promote healthy competition because they all require your undivided attention. What do most people want to feel when they're engaging in competition? They want to be in the zone. Well, you can't be in the zone and achieve that blissful state by focusing on others. You can only get there by focusing on yourself. Each of the 3 H's plays a significant role in helping competitors achieve their goals and perform at an optimal level because each of the 3 H's promotes healthy competition.

Let us begin with the first H, Heart. Earlier in this book I talked about being my own worst enemy. I told you how this type of behavior inhibited my performance. It was also toxic to my self-esteem. When you're not able to be your biggest cheerleader, your own best friend, you leave yourself vulnerable and wide open to criticism. While there's nothing wrong or unhealthy about constructive criticism, there is a form of criticism that is completely unhealthy. It is called negative criticism. This happened to me whenever I made the decision of surrounding myself with negative people. The problem was I would let these people tell me who I was or who I should be. Rather than connecting with myself and looking within, I chose to see what these negative people saw. This tore up my confidence, changed my behavior and completely smashed my sense of self. It led to my need to seek validation from others, when in reality that validation needed to come from within.

Having Heart requires confidence. It's knowing who you are. You've created a solid foundation that makes you less inclined to be affected by other's negativity. Not only do you have the ability to see things for how they are, you automatically reject needless energy suckers by standing up for who you are and what you believe in. I was driving the other day, and I started thinking about people in my life who had disappointed and hurt me. I immediately started to feel angry, but rather than expend energy on that anger in an unproductive and useless way, I began to feel strength, Heart and motivation that I was free from those situations and had overcome them.

What could have been a negative experience immediately turned into a positive and productive one in which I felt as though I was holding onto the reins of my own life. I was calling the shots. It was similar to that feeling I used to get when I had a bad day at school and jumped into my pool, my temple— no one could touch me. I was immune to it all. No one could make me feel less than. I was in control. The feeling I had was confidence. It was knowing who I am and loving who that person is. It was a calming feeling and I knew that everything was going to be okay, because my mind automatically shifted to my goals and my dreams. Rather than wasting my energy focusing on the judgement of others and their sometimes hurtful comments, I was focusing on myself. They weren't even a thought.

When you have Heart, your Heart and confidence are one. You're not cocky; you just are. You don't think of yourself in comparison to others. In fact, you're so involved in what you're doing that the actions of others are irrelevant. This in turn allows you to perform at an optimal level. When you have Heart, nothing else matters. You're in a place where you're able to excel. You're automatically engaging in healthy competition and by doing so, it is providing you with a competitive advantage.

Every goal I've ever achieved required more than one person. There was absolutely no way I could have achieved the things I did had I not had support from others. Dreams are like special secrets. We hold them close and whisper them to ourselves. Sometimes we refrain from sharing these dreams for fear that others might knock them down or convince us otherwise. This is why it is so gratifying when you can actually find someone with whom you can share your dreams, your secrets, and rather than laugh or scoff at you, they turn to you and smile and say, "I believe in you." You would not believe how much power those four simple words have, especially when they come from someone that you respect.

We all want someone to believe in us. While we know that believing in ourselves comes first, having someone else to support us allows for those times when we're faced with self-doubt or are feeling completely overwhelmed. It wasn't until toward the end of my competitive swimming career that I began swimming for the most supportive and inspiring coach. It's a shame that gift was not granted earlier, but I'm grateful nonetheless that I was given that gift at all. Having a coach who recognizes your work ethic, nurtures your talent, and believes in your ability to succeed, automatically boosts your confidence. It's actually a scientific fact. There have been studies that have proven that people feel much better about their lives and themselves when they feel emotionally connected to others. Positive reinforcement is just another way for people to be connected. One can even argue that the connection is much stronger or more special when it's based on excelling at something that is so close to your heart. Being supported creates a competitive advantage because it breeds a positive environment in which healthy competition can live and breathe. Healthy competition gets us to challenge ourselves, and can result in some of the best performances of all time. If you look at people who excel in their areas of expertise you will see a common theme, and that theme will most likely be positive reinforcement from someone other than themselves.

Having Heart requires a sense of self. It means loving yourself for exactly who you are despite your faults. It allows you to free up excess energy. Rather than focusing your energy on perfecting or changing yourself for your perceived faults, you look at how you can be the best version of yourself. You're mindful and aware of your thoughts and how they affect your actions. When you start feeling yucky and wish to put an end to those type of emotions, you look within. Since how you think affects how you feel which in turn dictates your actions, your emotional intelligence level is high. You're more comfortable with your own thoughts and you're better able to get a grip on your emotions and actions because you've learned how to understand yourself and your feelings. You've learned not to run away from your emotions because in doing so, you've found that not only do they not go away, but they require energy that can be better spent on you.

Heart provides a competitor with the fuel, the energy, the motivation to be better. Having Heart doesn't just mean that you care. It's more than caring. You're 100% invested. You also hold yourself accountable for your actions. You recognize your mistakes and see them as opportunities to learn. When you fail, you get right back up. Why? Because you have Heart. You notice the people you have in your life who feed you with positivity rather than negativity and build upon those relationships. You know that you can't do this alone. Having Heart means finding someone who supports you that you can confide in and share your dreams with. Having Heart means that your focus is on you but not in an egotistical way. You're aware of your sense of self but it does not define you—it just is. Having Heart means you're building your dreams and working toward them. You're engaging in healthy competition.

Having Heart also means standing your ground even if it's just to show yourself that you can. I mentioned earlier about how my dad used to joke about me being the number-one ball buster and how I kind of liked this about me. Let's be honest, I REALLY liked this about me. I didn't see this as a negative at all. In fact, my brother's friends once asked my dad if he was worried about me dating guys and my dad simply replied, "Dani's going to do what Dani wants to do, when she wants to do it." My brother's friends laughed because they knew enough about me to know this fact to be true. I of course laughed when my brother's friend shared the story with me later because I saw my stubbornness as a strength. I saw it as having Heart.

In order for one to be competitive, one must be persistent, and being persistent requires one to have Heart. It means being disciplined enough to know that success comes when hard work is invested over a significant period of time. Despite what some may think when they see others succeed, rest assured that their success was not obtained instantaneously. The reason we think it occurred overnight is because no one shows us all of the hard work and effort that went into working toward their goal. If this information were shared, we'd probably find it cumbersome and overwhelming. In addition, these individuals have so much Heart that they often make everything that they do look easy.

Sometimes in life it takes failure for us to succeed. What I mean is that it's quite easy for people to get discouraged and lose hope when they're working toward a goal and they feel like it's never going to happen, or they find themselves stumbling more than once. When this happens they're thinking, "What's the point? Why not just quit?" The answer is, because quitting is easy. It takes a stubborn, persistent person with Heart to achieve great things. When we're solid in our decisions and nothing can change our minds, working toward a goal seems feasible. Heart is attitude. It is what fuels a healthy competitive spirit.

The second H is Hunger. Hunger is a big one. Hunger is the thing you see when you turn on the television to watch a game and notice one basketball team seems to want it more. It's this obvious unspoken energy fans can sense and get swept up in because it's intoxicating. Hunger is where motivation and desire meet. It's when every fiber of your being yearns for more. You want success and you want it badly. You find yourself more invested than ever, and you can't quite put your finger on it, but you love the feeling and hope it never leaves.

Earlier in this book, I talked about getting into the zone and the importance of creating a competitive state where people can challenge themselves. I also mentioned how getting into the zone cannot exist if someone is not pushing their boundaries. Hunger and being in the zone live in the same universe. They coexist. Hunger and being in the zone take us to a level where one can feel as though they're having an out-of-body experience. They feel this way due to a sense of euphoria, a feeling they've never quite felt before. Everything seems effortless. Why? Because of the Hunger.

Hunger requires taking risks, venturing outside of your comfort zone. If one maintains the same routine after they've excelled, they're not asking more of themselves. When people become complacent and refrain from pushing themselves, they cannot be expected to perform at a higher level the next time that they compete. There comes a point in time where the workout you're doing no longer becomes sufficient. This occurred when my coach wanted me to increase my training and incorporate a morning swim to compliment my afternoon workouts. Morning workouts were at 4:30 am. I know—most normal people were sleeping. My dad used to drive me to practice. It would be pitch black. While part of me dreaded jumping into that cold pool water, those morning workouts made me stronger. Besides, no one wakes up to train at 4:30 am unless they're hungry.

The point of creating goals and challenging ourselves is that it requires us to be hungry, to engage in something we enjoy that doesn't feel like work. When I was training for Junior Nationals in the 200 meter butterfly, I swam in what we used to refer to as a practice meet. A practice meet means that you train right through the competition as opposed to tapering or lightening your workout before the swim meet. The intent is to practice like you're in a workout but do so in a more competitive environment. Sometimes swimmers even wear drag, which is excess swimsuits or tights and shorts so that they can make the race even more challenging for themselves. The philosophy behind this is that by continually challenging yourself while in training mode, when it comes time to taper and perform at an important swim meet, you'll feel significantly lighter in the water and glide more easily in your stroke.

I was at a training meet and had signed up to swim the 1,000 yard freestyle. Since it is permissible when competing in a freestyle event to swim a stroke other than freestyle when competing, I decided to take a risk and swim butterfly instead. While I was 100% nervous, I was also excited. I wanted to test myself and see if I could really do it and I did! I was hungry and my Hunger served me well.

Hunger makes competing more exciting. It allows us to push ourselves to achieve things we may have never thought we were capable of. It creates an inner fire. It makes us come alive because it feeds off our emotions by converting them into positive energy that we can use to excel. Hunger is where happiness lives, even if we're not conscious of it. It's where healthy competition lives because it creates possibilities and opportunities. It sees what's possible as opposed to what isn't. It creates such a positive aura that it's amazing how much of a competitive advantage those with Hunger have.

The last of the 3 H's is Hard Work. Hard Work comes much easier to someone when Heart and Hunger exist. There's more incentive, more inspiration. You're not just going through the motions. You're genuinely engaged and interested.

Hard Work is necessary. While your talent might provide you with more of a competitive advantage, it doesn't win you golds. Just look at Michael Phelps.

His body was created for swimming. His stroke, turns and ability to be versatile and swim multiple events at the Olympics and win is uncanny. He surpassed Mark Spitz's record. After Beijing, Phelps took some time off from swimming. He most certainly deserved it. The thing is that after having taken that time out, Michael Phelps' performances in the pool didn't exactly mirror Beijing. Why? Because that's what happens when you step away. This is why some competitors burn out before quitting. They're afraid to take that break. They know just how important Hard Work is and are reluctant to give it up.

When I was at the top of my game in the pool and in the office, I was working like a maniac. I put everything I had into everything I did. At work, I did so much that when the company eventually increased our department's head count, I was rewarded with a new Manager to help me out with my intense work load. The new Manager pulled me aside and asked me how was it possible for me to have done all the work that I did before he came aboard. I did it because I had Heart and Hunger, and was willing to do the Hard Work. When you want something as badly as I did, you'll be surprised at how far you'll go to make things happen and how hard you're willing to work for it.

When you're working hard, you find yourself automatically seeking new information and new ways of doing things. My nana used to say you know you're dead when you stop wanting to learn. She was right. Whether metaphorically or physically speaking, it doesn't matter. The minute you decide to stop working hard and become complacent with what you have, is the moment you decide that you no longer wish to invest in yourself.

The desire to learn can be a motivational tool. To continue to learn is essential if we are to achieve our goals. We pursue new information every time we challenge ourselves and chase our dreams. We do this by learning how to perfect our stroke, how to communicate better in the office, how to run faster and so on. We seek new information because we are not complacent. We want to grow and we cannot do this without maintaining our curiosity and working hard.

The most important thing is that you not cheat yourself out of your Hard Work. Make sure that while you're working, you are present. There's no point in showing up physically if you're not going to be there mentally. That's a lazy way of competing and no one gets away with that forever. It's both feet in, or nothing at all. By dedicating yourself and putting forth effort, you're automatically engaging in healthy competitive behavior because your focus is on you. It's all about your growth, not others. You start creating small short-term goals along the way to help keep you motivated. You're not easily distracted because your focus is on the work. It's that simple.

When you have the 3 H's—Heart, Hunger and Hard Work—anything is possible. I call it the perfect tri. Everything aligns and it's all systems go. The 3 H's are something I saw in every competitive situation I witnessed when I was making the decision of whether to quit swimming or not. The reason I chose to walk away was because while I was still willing to Work Hard, my Heart was not in it. I was no longer hungry. I no longer felt that inner fire, that motivation to be the best. It just wasn't there, and there was no way I could even begin to fake it. While it made me happy to be able to look back and reflect on how I felt when I was on top of my swimming game, I knew that those same emotions were no longer there. I was no longer having fun. It made me sad to think about it, but it was more of a reality check than anything.

If you're not having fun, what's the point? While one can have fun causing mischief, I'm specifically referring to the kind of fun required when one engages in healthy competitive behavior. It is the kind of fun that brings about pure enjoyment. It is the kind of fun when excitement exists and it makes you kind of giddy. It is also the kind of fun that gives you a sense of peace. It removes all of life's daily stresses and allows you to be free, almost childlike. Remember the feeling you had when you were a kid playing games in the neighborhood? Remember how some people took it so seriously while others laughed and giggled? Who do you think was more inclined to perform better in that experience? The child who was tense and serious or the one who was loose and light-hearted? I'm going to go with the latter.

I always swam better when I was free spirited, when I was having fun. Truth be told, that's probably why I swam so much better in workouts than at swim meets. I would have fun when I was practicing. I would be excited to jump in the pool at workout because I was jumping into my temple, my sanctuary. I also found myself goofing around with my team-mates, which made me laugh and smile. It always made practice that much more enjoyable. It wasn't that I was goofing around to the point where I was slacking off. It was being able not to take things so seriously while still giving it my all and having the ability to maintain my focus during each set.

It is my experience that when things stop becoming fun, we find ourselves losing our focus and trying less. It is when we are having fun—however we define it—that we're in the right mindset to be motivated and inspired. It is during these times that the healthiest form of competition can occur.

Conclusion

Think of the 3 H's as a formula:

**Heart + Hunger + Hard Work =
Healthy Competition**

One can even argue that it's really 4 H's as opposed to 3. The reason I call it the 3 H's and not the 4 H's is because without Heart, Hunger and Hard Work, you do not have Healthy Competition. If you start looking around at various types of competition, you'll begin to notice that the people who perform at an optimal level all have the 3 H's, Heart, Hunger and Hard Work. Look at Steven Spielberg, Oprah Winfrey, Jon Stewart, and Michael Phelps— all 3 H's were present. These extraordinary individuals achieved a level of remarkable success that once seemed impossible. Coincidence? I think not. I've seen the exact same thing when I've listened to artists like Taylor Swift and Beyoncé talk about their music. In each situation Heart, Hunger and Hard Work were clearly visible, but so were their attitudes. All of these individuals approached competition in a healthy way. They welcomed it.

I was reading something the other day on how we drive ourselves crazy making decisions. I admit to being indecisive at times. Do I go to the gym or watch TV? Do I eat the salad or the candy bar? In response to the fact that people tend to feel overwhelmed by all the choices that they have to make in life, the article suggested narrowing your options by turning the picking process into a sports bracket. In other words, it would be helpful to divide your choices into groups, select a winner from each group and then line up your top selects, and choose from those which one will be your ultimate winner. I laughed when I read this. The article had a point. Every time we make a choice, we stack options against one another and make them compete for us. It's funny when you think about it. The apple competes against the orange and the orange wins because I chose it over the apple.

It's amazing how much of a role competition plays in our daily lives. The best part is that we can learn to have fun with it. Just like choosing one fruit over the other doesn't require unnecessary energy or solicit jealousy, hatred or anger, we don't need to add those factors to our other forms of daily competition. It's all relative. While some competing decisions are not as serious as others, does it really matter? I think what matters most is that we learn how to conserve our energy so that we can use it wisely. We can use it to our advantage.

Had I not discovered Heart, Hunger and Hard Work, the decision to quit swimming would have been more brutal than it was. I would have had no idea what questions to ask myself to guide me in making a choice I would not later regret.

It wasn't until much later in life that I had my second epiphany as it relates to the 3 H theory. That epiphany was Healthy Competition. It was a delayed reaction as I did not realize how much of a role healthy competition had played in my life and how connected it was to Heart, Hunger and Hard Work. It was as if the equation (Heart + Hunger + Hard Work = Healthy Competition) had been staring me in the face for years and I had just chosen to see it. Perhaps my observations and my experiences had made me much more mindful than I had been, so it wasn't until now that it presented itself. It doesn't matter. What matters is that I now have a formula for success for the next goal I set, and it is going to make it much easier this time for me to achieve it.

When it comes to competition the things to do versus the things not to do, have become clear to me. No more expending energy on my competitors. See them for who they are and observe them. Don't get emotionally invested. Invest those emotions in yourself. Be positive. Nurture your dreams. When you get defeated or feel as though you've failed, remember that those are the moments when you can learn the most and have the best opportunity to grow. Healthy competition requires effort, but it can also be exhilarating.

In life it's hard to keep the little things from bothering us. Sometimes they just attach themselves like barnacles of negativity, and we feel as though we cannot shake them. When this happens, I suggest retreating to your own corner and chilling out. Once you've cooled down, revisit your thoughts, and examine them so that you can find out which emotion was controlling you so that you can address it.

When I swam competitively, I had Heart because I had confidence. I knew who I was and had a wonderful coach who supported me. I had Hunger because I was encouraged to be hungry and perform my best. I had Hard Work and it wasn't just acknowledged, it was encouraged. I had a healthy competitive environment, and in turn I became a healthy competitor.

Looking back, I wish I had arrived at my theory a long time ago. It would have helped me. It would have made me more confident in my potential and helped me to tune out distractions. In the end, life is what it is and I am okay with that. Just as I say to learn from your mistakes, I too have learned from mine.

If you were to revisit the definition of *competition* now, would you define it the same way as *Merriam's Webster Dictionary* or would you choose to redefine it? Perhaps it's just waiting to be rediscovered, waiting for new eyes and a new perspective.

If healthy competition means challenging yourself to be more innovative, performing at an optimal level and surpassing your expectations, why not push yourself to take the healthy competitive challenge? Embrace competition's finer points and leave the rest for never. Inspiration and positivity come from within. We just need a healthy competitor who will help bring out the best in us. That healthy competitor can be you.

I'd like to invite you to take the healthy competitive challenge. Be more mindful of your behavior and see how competition affects you in your everyday life. Try to find ways to engage in healthy competition;

the kind of healthy competition we discussed that makes you smile and feel good about yourself. If you'd like to share your story, you can post it on **lifegameonbook.com**. You can also go to *Dani's Dictionary* and define the word *competition*. It will be our own version of *Urban Dictionary*. I'm anxious to hear what you have to say. I think everyone's perspective and insight will be helpful and enlightening. The goal is to spread the message. That message is healthy competition and how we can all embrace it.

About The Author

Dani Golden took her first steps in a pool and it was there that she discovered her love of swimming. Having grown up swimming competitively, Dani has had a lot of practice in dealing with competition.

Dani graduated from the School of Journalism at the University of Colorado at Boulder. An Advertising major, she minored in Sociology and has found herself fascinated by human behavior. She traveled around the world as she did a semester abroad. This humbled her and provided her with a variety of perspectives she has carried with her to this day. After graduating college, Dani pursued a career in Advertising and Marketing. Exposed to two extremely competitive industries, her knowledge and awareness of competition continued to grow.

Throughout Dani's life, she has noticed a common theme: competition. She looked back on her life and noticed how much competition had affected her both personally and professionally. Her desire to understand her competitive spirit motivated her to write *LIFE. GAME ON! A Competitor's Guide.* In this book she shares the knowledge she has gained from her experiences to encourage others to discover their passion and find their fun.

dani@dgencinitas.com
lifegameonbook.com
danigolden.com

www.ingramcontent.com/pod-product-compliance
Lightning Source LLC
La Vergne TN
LVHW021350080426
835508LV00020B/2201